This Book Belongs To

○┄┄┄┄┄┄┄┄┄┄┄┄○
○┄┄┄┄┄┄┄┄┄┄┄┄○

COPYRIGHT © 2025

All rights reserved.

No part of this book, including illustrations or interactive content, may be copied, reproduced, or shared in any form without the publisher's written permission, except for brief excerpts used in reviews or as allowed by copyright law.

Author
Ethan Turnea

Add More Fun!

YOU CAN ENJOY THIS JOKE BOOK WITH THE FOLLOWING RULES:

1. CHOOSE YOUR TEAM OR GO HEAD-TO-HEAD.
2. SIT FACING EACH OTHER AND MAKE EYE CONTACT.
3. TAKE TURNS READING JOKES OUT LOUD.
4. ADD EXTRA FUN WITH SILLY FACES, FUNNY SOUNDS, OR WACKY GESTURES!
5. WHEN YOUR OPPONENT LAUGHS, YOU EARN A POINT.
6. THE FIRST TO 3 POINTS WINS!

LET THE LAUGHTER BEGIN AND MAY THE FUNNIEST PLAYER WIN!

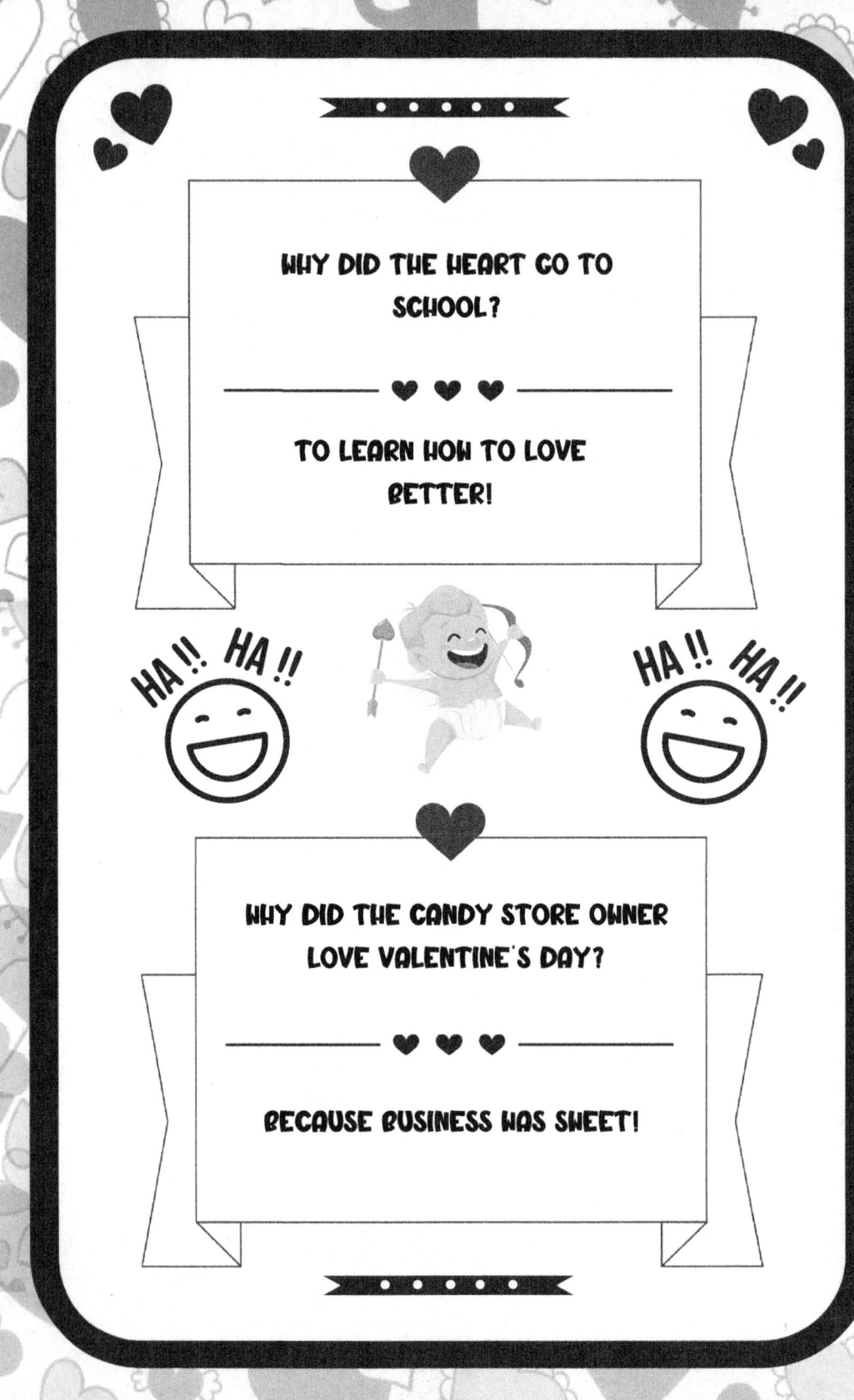

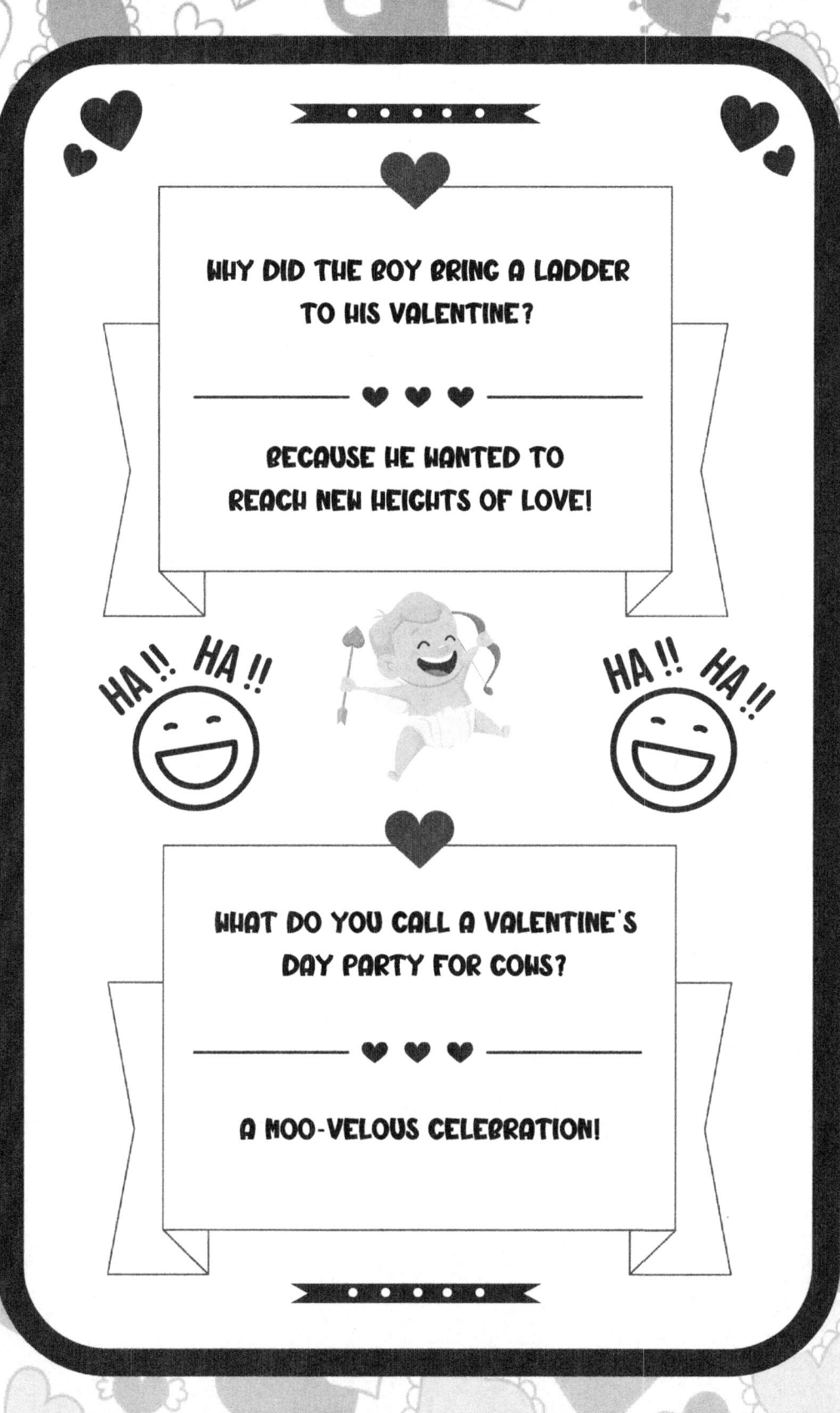

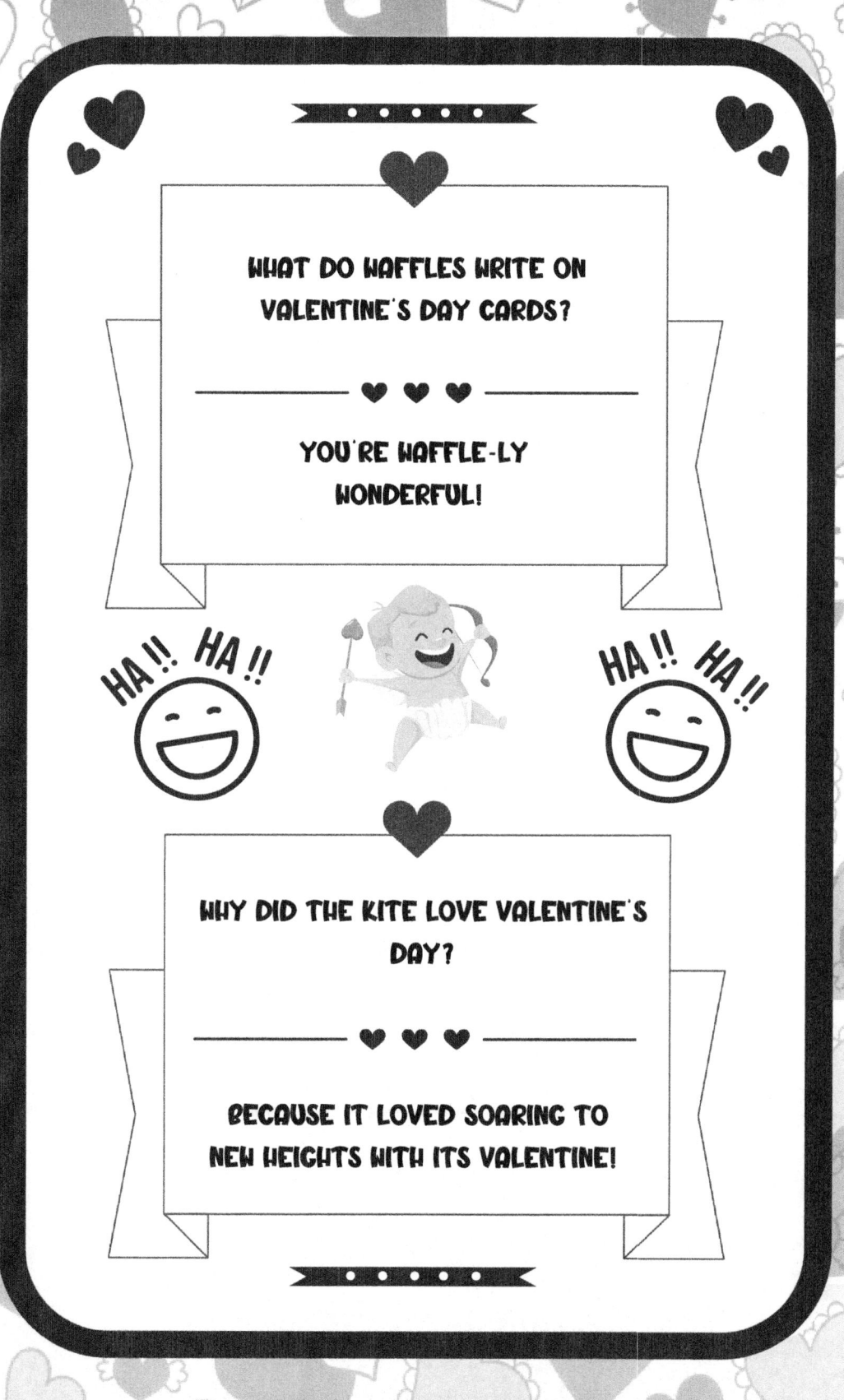

WHAT DID THE DRAGON SAY TO ITS VALENTINE?

♥ ♥ ♥

YOU SET MY HEART ON FIRE!

HA!! HA!!

HA!! HA!!

WHY DID THE SKATEBOARD GIVE A VALENTINE?

♥ ♥ ♥

BECAUSE IT WAS ROLLING IN LOVE!

WHAT'S A SOCCER BALL'S VALENTINE'S DAY WISH?

♥ ♥ ♥

TO FIND SOMEONE WHO KICKS IT JUST RIGHT!

HA!! HA!!   HA!! HA!!

WHY DID THE PIZZA PROPOSE ON VALENTINE'S DAY?

♥ ♥ ♥

BECAUSE IT FOUND ITS PERFECT TOPPING!

WHAT DID THE GLITTER SAY TO THE VALENTINE CARD?

YOU MAKE EVERYTHING SPARKLE!

WHAT'S A BEE'S FAVORITE LOVE SONG?

CAN'T STOP BUZZING ABOUT YOU!

WHY DID THE ELEPHANT BRING CHOCOLATES?

♥ ♥ ♥

BECAUSE IT NEVER FORGETS SOMEONE IT LOVES!

HA!! HA!!   HA!! HA!!

WHAT DID ONE MARSHMALLOW SAY TO THE OTHER?

♥ ♥ ♥

YOU'RE MY S'MORE LOVE!

WHY DID THE BUTTERFLY FALL IN LOVE?

♥ ♥ ♥

IT FOUND SOMEONE WHO MADE ITS HEART FLUTTER!

HA!! HA!!   HA!! HA!!

WHAT'S A RACE CAR'S FAVORITE VALENTINE'S MESSAGE?

♥ ♥ ♥

YOU DRIVE ME CRAZY... IN A GOOD WAY!

WHY DID THE MAGICIAN SEND A VALENTINE?

♥ ♥ ♥

TO SAY, "YOU'VE GOT ME UNDER YOUR SPELL!"

WHAT DID ONE FORTUNE COOKIE SAY TO THE OTHER?

♥ ♥ ♥

YOU'RE MY LUCKY CHARM!

WHY DID THE ASTRONAUT BLUSH ON VALENTINE'S DAY?

♥ ♥ ♥

BECAUSE IT WAS OVER THE MOON IN LOVE

WHAT DO YOU CALL A VAMPIRE'S VALENTINE'S DAY CARD?

♥ ♥ ♥

A FANG-TASTIC MESSAGE OF LOVE!

WHAT DID THE MERMAID WRITE ON HER VALENTINE?

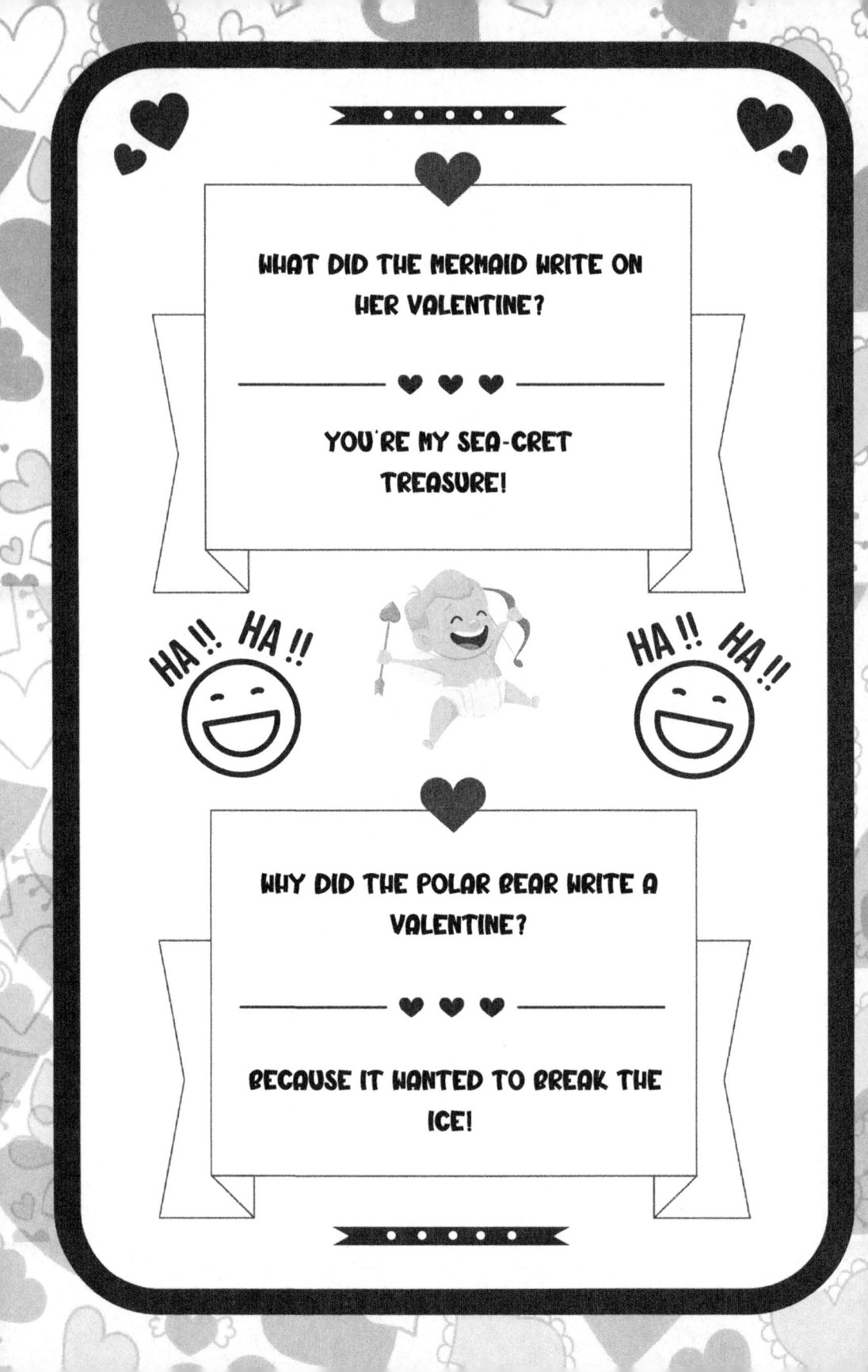

♥ ♥ ♥

YOU'RE MY SEA-CRET TREASURE!

WHY DID THE POLAR BEAR WRITE A VALENTINE?

♥ ♥ ♥

BECAUSE IT WANTED TO BREAK THE ICE!

WHAT'S A SOCCER NET'S VALENTINE'S WISH?

♥ ♥ ♥

TO CATCH SOMEONE SPECIAL!

WHAT DID THE MOON SAY TO THE STARS?

♥ ♥ ♥

I LOVE YOU TO INFINITY AND BEYOND!

WHY DID THE KOALA SEND A VALENTINE?

♥ ♥ ♥

BECAUSE IT WAS CLINGING TO LOVE!

HA!! HA!!   HA!! HA!!

WHAT'S A TRAIN'S VALENTINE'S DAY MESSAGE?

♥ ♥ ♥

YOU CHOO-CHOO-CHOOSE ME EVERY TIME!

WHAT DID THE CACTUS SAY TO ITS VALENTINE?

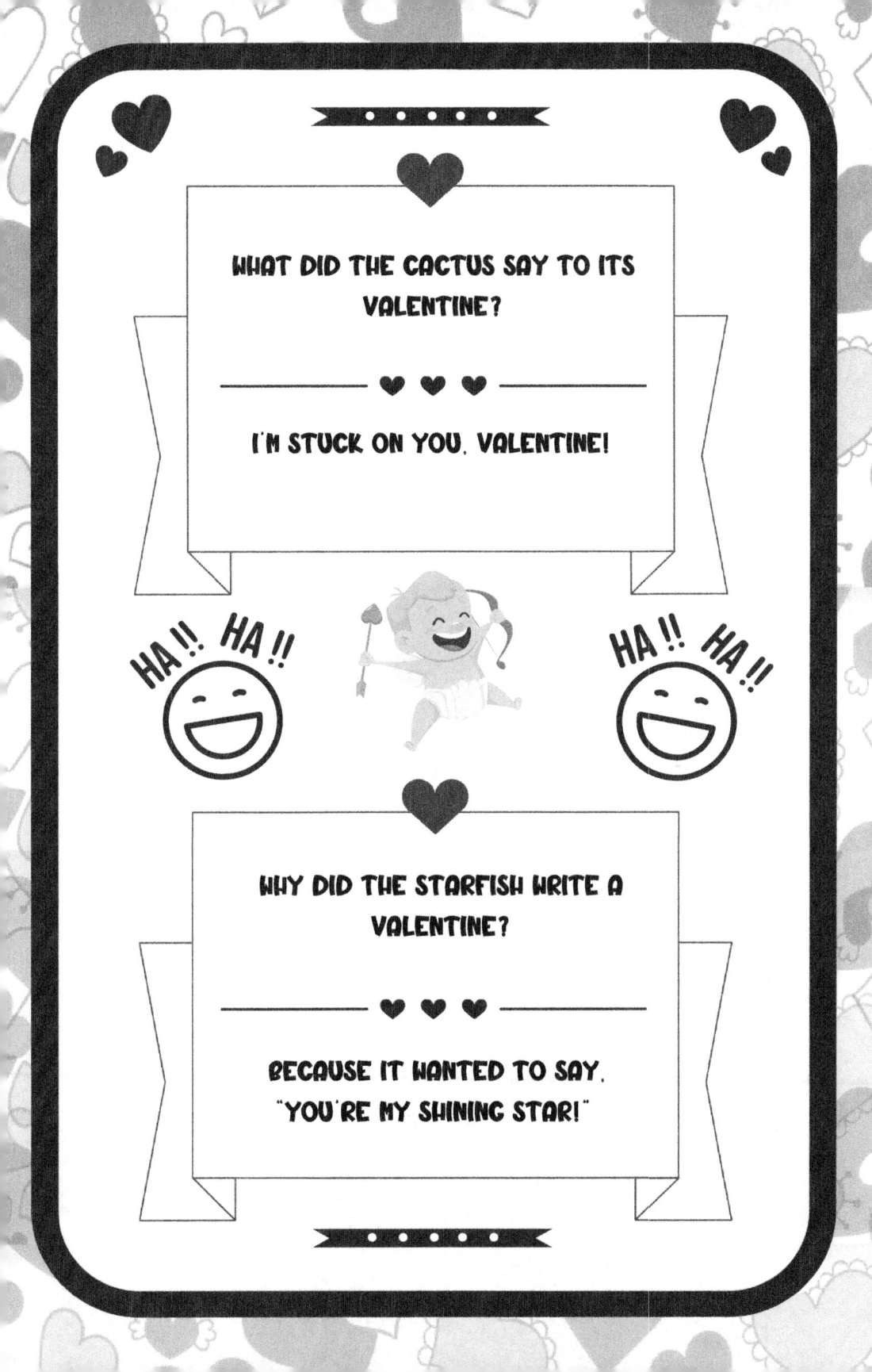

♥ ♥ ♥

I'M STUCK ON YOU, VALENTINE!

HA!! HA!!   HA!! HA!!

WHY DID THE STARFISH WRITE A VALENTINE?

♥ ♥ ♥

BECAUSE IT WANTED TO SAY, "YOU'RE MY SHINING STAR!"

WHAT'S A MAGICIAN'S FAVORITE VALENTINE'S TRICK?

❤ ❤ ❤

MAKING HEARTS APPEAR OUT OF THIN AIR!

WHY DID THE JELLYFISH FALL IN LOVE?

❤ ❤ ❤

IT COULDN'T RESIST THE ELECTRIC SPARK!

WHAT'S A POPCORN KERNEL'S VALENTINE'S DAY WISH?

♥ ♥ ♥

TO POP INTO SOMEONE'S HEART!

HA!! HA!! HA!! HA!!

WHY DID THE ROBOT FEEL HAPPY ON VALENTINE'S DAY?

♥ ♥ ♥

BECAUSE IT FOUND THE PERFECT MATCH TO PLUG INTO ITS HEART!

WHAT DID THE RACING CAR SAY TO ITS VALENTINE?

♥ ♥ ♥

YOU'RE MY FINISH LINE!

WHAT DO PIRATES SAY ON VALENTINE'S DAY?

♥ ♥ ♥

YOU ARRR MY TREASURE!

WHY DID THE SANDWICH WRITE A VALENTINE?

♥ ♥ ♥

BECAUSE IT WANTED TO SPREAD THE LOVE!

HA!! HA!!   HA!! HA!!

WHAT'S A SNOWFLAKE'S VALENTINE'S DAY WISH?

♥ ♥ ♥

TO LAND SOFTLY IN SOMEONE'S HEART!

WHY DID THE PENCIL BLUSH ON VALENTINE'S DAY?

♥ ♥ ♥

BECAUSE IT WAS DRAWING HEARTS ALL DAY!

HA!! HA!!   HA!! HA!!

WHAT DO FROGS GIVE ON VALENTINE'S DAY?

♥ ♥ ♥

HOP-PY HUGS!

WHAT DID THE CLOCK SAY TO THE WATCH?

❤ ❤ ❤

YOU MAKE MY TIME FLY BY!

HA!! HA!!

HA!! HA!!

WHY DID THE RAINBOW SEND A VALENTINE?

❤ ❤ ❤

TO BRIGHTEN UP SOMEONE'S CLOUDY DAY!

WHAT DID THE FLAMINGO SAY ON VALENTINE'S DAY?

♥ ♥ ♥

LET'S FLAMINGLE AND FALL IN LOVE!

WHAT DO ELVES GIVE ON VALENTINE'S DAY?

♥ ♥ ♥

MAGICAL LOVE NOTES!